MW01079657

# Telling Time

## with the Judy® Clock

### Second Grade

Carson-Dellosa Publishing, LLC
Greensboro, North Carolina

**Credits**

Content Editor: Jennifer B. Stith
Copy Editor: Julie B. Killian
Layout Design: Lori Jackson
Cover Design: Nick Greenwood

Carson-Dellosa Publishing, LLC
PO Box 35665
Greensboro, NC 27425 USA
carsondellosa.com

ISBN 978-1-62057-346-4

# Table of Contents

This resource is designed to foster the development of students' concepts of time. Using the Judy® Clock* helps engage the process skills necessary for measuring time in the real world. This amazing "time tool" gives students hands-on experience with all of the workings of a real clock! Students will see how the gears inside make the hands move in conjunction with each other around the clock face.

Before introducing students to the activities in this book, allow students to explore their clocks along with you as you manipulate the hands and compare the Judy Clock to your classroom wall clock. Then, when students engage in the book's activities, they will use their Judy Clocks to learn the parts of a clock, measure time, and develop an understanding of the concept of elapsed time.

While completing the activities in *Telling Time with the Judy Clock* for second grade, students will use the clock to

- understand and use vocabulary related to time;
- tell time to the quarter hour and five minute intervals;
- understand elapsed time; and
- know when to use am and pm.

Initially, introduce all of the games and activities in this book to the whole class. Then, once students understand the directions for the activities and games, have them work in pairs, small groups, or individually at learning centers. You may also want to laminate the cards and game boards for extended use.


*Judy Clocks are available in various sizes with digital and/or analog times at your local school supply dealer or at *carsondellosa.com*.

## Telling Time Three Ways

*Materials: Judy Clock, construction paper, scissors*

Introduce quarter hours with this easy activity. First, cut out a construction paper circle the same size as the face of the Judy Clock. Cut the circle into fourths. Cover the face of the Judy Clock with the paper circle. Show students how the clock face forms a circle. As you remove each fourth of the paper, help students discover that four quarters make up the clock face. Then, display a time on the hour such as 6:00. Ask, "What time does the clock show?" Then, begin moving the minute hand and counting by fives until you set the clock to 6:15. Tell students that this time is also 15 minutes after 6 or quarter after (or past) 6. Repeat this activity several times to let students practice reading quarter hours three ways.

Challenge students by having volunteers set the two times on the clock and ask the questions themselves.

## Time Tag

*Materials: Judy Clock, coin*

Reinforce quarter hours with this active indoor game. Divide students into two teams. Have each team choose a "tagger." Have the taggers stand about four feet away from you and the teams sit on either side of you. Flip a coin to decide which team goes first. Set the Judy Clock to a time on the hour. Have the first player on the team set the time to quarter after the hour. If the player sets the clock correctly, the tagger for that team takes one big step toward you. If the player sets the clock incorrectly, the tagger does not move. Teams take turns setting the Judy Clock and trying to advance their taggers. The first tagger to tag you wins.

After playing the game several times, challenge students by not setting the hour first and having them set the Judy Clock to the quarter hour without your help.

# Arms and "Hands"

*Materials: Judy Clock*

Review time to the quarter hour and get students to exercise with this activity. Choose a student to lead arm exercises. Then, have students stand and form rows in front of the leader, standing arms-width apart from each other. Tell the leader to set an hour on the clock and call out the time. Then, ask students to simulate the time by holding their arms like the hands of the clock.

Lead the class in counting by fives. Have the leader move the minute hand and students move their arms "around the clock" until they reach 15 minutes after the hour. At that point, call out the time. Then, continue leading everyone in counting by fives until they reach 45 minutes after the hour. At that point, call out the time again.

As students progress, have them call out the time with you.

# Wake Up!

*Materials: Judy Clock*

Set a time to the quarter hour on the Judy Clock. Have students read the time. Next, choose three volunteers. Have the rest of the class sit on the floor and cover their eyes. While their eyes are closed, silently choose one of the volunteers to move the clock hands to show a new quarter hour time.

Have volunteers call out, "Wake up! Wake up! Who moved the hands?" Have students open their eyes and try to guess which of the three volunteers set the time. The class gets three tries. The student who guesses correctly and reads the correct time gets to choose two other students to set the clock with him. If no one guesses correctly, the three volunteers repeat the game.

## Tracking Time

*Materials: Judy Clock, minute timer, paper, pencil*

This activity provides a fun way to help students grasp the 15-minute and 45-minute time periods. At the beginning of the day, ask students what they think they could do in 15 minutes, such as brush their teeth or get dressed. Then, ask what they could do in 45 minutes, such as eat dinner or play a board game. Tell them that you will be setting a minute timer throughout the day to signal 15-minute and 45-minute time periods.

Start at the beginning of the school day by setting the Judy Clock to 9:00. Set the minute timer for 15 minutes. When the timer goes off, set the Judy Clock to the time and list the kinds of activities students did in that time period.

Wait for 10:00 and set the Judy Clock again. Then, set the minute timer for 45 minutes. When the timer goes off, stop and list the things that students accomplished in those 45 minutes. Compare the two lists and discuss the similarities and differences.

As an extension, ask students to time activities at home and have their families help them make lists of the things that took them 15 minutes to do and the activities that took them 45 minutes to do. Encourage students to share their lists.

## Judy, May We?

*Materials: Judy Clock*

Have students stand with partners, side by side, in a row on the playground. Hold the Judy Clock and stand about 10 feet away from the class. The first pair of students says, "Judy, may we take one giant step toward you?" Set the Judy Clock to a quarter hour. The first pair of players must call out the time. If correct, say, "Yes, you may." If incorrect, say, "No, you may not." Then, it is the next pair's turn. The first pair to tag you wins.

# Snapping Time

*Materials: Judy Clock*

Choose a student to be the leader and hold the Judy Clock. Have students sit in front of the leader. Review with students that when the minute hand points to the 3, it is 15 minutes after (or past) the hour. Demonstrate on the board that there are three different ways to write this time—6:15, 15 minutes after 6, and quarter past 6. Tell the leader to set an hour on the clock and say the time. Then, have her call out, "Snap!" While the rest of the group snaps the seconds, the leader moves the minute hand to the 3. Then, invite the leader to choose a classmate to say the new time in one of the three ways. If the classmate is correct, he becomes the new leader and sets a new time on the clock.

# Time Master

*Materials: Judy Clock, handkerchief or other blindfold*

Choose a student to be the Time Master. Then, have students sit in a circle around the Time Master. Blindfold a volunteer. Have the Time Master set the Judy Clock to a quarter hour. The blindfolded student gets three chances to guess the time. He can ask for a clue before each guess. The Time Master can ask any student to give a clue such as, "It is a time before 12:00 and after 1:00." If the blindfolded student guesses correctly within three tries, he becomes the next Time Master, and a new student is blindfolded. If the blindfolded student guesses incorrectly, he returns to the circle, and a new student is blindfolded.

Five...ten...

## Three-Quarter Time

*Materials: Judy Clock*

Set the Judy Clock to 5:45. Say to students, "When the minute hand points to the 9, it is three quarters after the hour. There are four different ways to say this time—5:45, 45 minutes after 5, 15 minutes before 6, and quarter to 6." Set the time on the hour. Have students count by fives with you until the minute hand reaches the 9. Lead students in saying the time in four different ways. Set the time on the hour again and slowly move the minute hand to the three-quarter hour. Ask who can read the time. The student with the first correct answer gets to set the new time and choose someone else to read it. Repeat this game several times to get students used to reading three-quarter time.

## Down the Rabbit Hole

*Materials: Judy Clock, index cards with the numbers 1–12, hour hand cut from card stock, minute hand cut from card stock*

This game is played like the classic game of Duck, Duck, Goose. On separate index cards, write the 24 quarter hours on the clock. Then, follow these directions:

1. Have students sit in a circle and give each student a card.

2. Choose a student to be the "rabbit."

3. While you are setting the Judy Clock to a quarter hour, the rabbit walks around the outside of the circle saying the famous line from *Alice's Adventures in Wonderland* by Lewis Carroll, "I'm late, I'm late, for a very important date."

4. Call out the time you set. The student who has the card that matches the time tries to tag the rabbit who is running around the circle to get to the runner's spot (or "rabbit hole") before being tagged.

5. If the rabbit is tagged, he sits in the center of the circle and chooses a new rabbit. If the rabbit gets to the rabbit hole before being tagged, the runner becomes the new rabbit.

6. Each time a new rabbit goes to the center of the circle, the old rabbit gets to join the circle.

# Tic-Tac-Time Game

*Materials: Judy Clock, copies of the Tic-Tac-Time Grid (page 10), pencils, buttons or plastic counters (optional)*

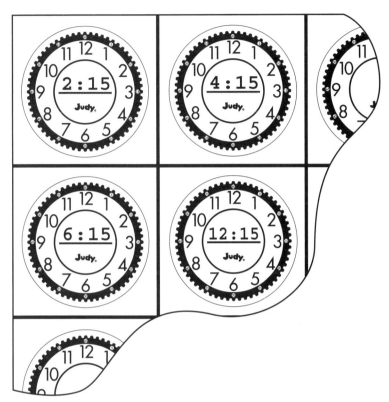

Try this modified version of Tic-Tac-Toe to provide practice in telling time to the quarter hour. Divide students into pairs and give one Tic-Tac-Time Grid to each pair. Have students write the times listed at the bottom of the page in the center of different Judy Clocks on the Tic-Tac-Time Grid. Times will be repeated more than once. Encourage students to randomly write the times on the clocks.

Help students decide which partner will go first (for example, the person with the longest first name or the person with the shortest last name). Then, set the Judy Clock to a quarter hour. Call out the time. The first player finds the matching time on the Tic-Tac-Time Grid and marks an *X* on the box. (You may have students use buttons or plastic counters instead.) Then, set the Judy Clock to a different quarter hour. The next player finds the matching time and marks an *O* on the corresponding box. The first player to get three in a row across, down, or diagonally wins and calls out, "Tic-Tac-Time!"

Challenge students by having winners try to get four, five, or six in a row. As an alternative, change the times listed on the grid to half-hour or three-quarter-hour times.

Name_____

# Tic-Tac-Time

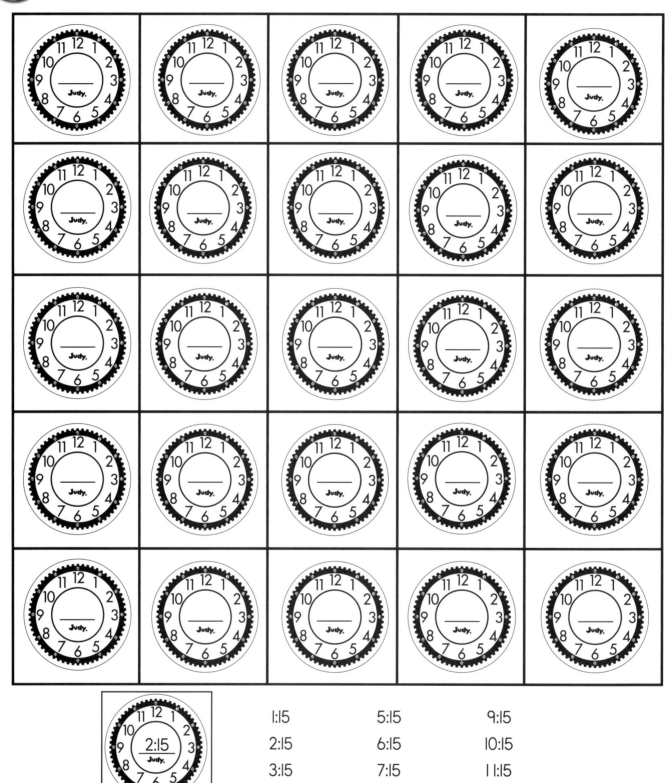

Example

| | | |
|---|---|---|
| 1:15 | 5:15 | 9:15 |
| 2:15 | 6:15 | 10:15 |
| 3:15 | 7:15 | 11:15 |
| 4:15 | 8:15 | 12:15 |

# Quarter Hours

Just as four quarters are in a dollar, four quarters are in an hour.

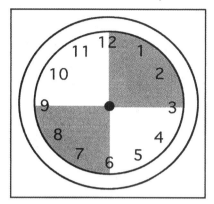

This is quarter past the hour.                This is quarter to the hour.

Draw hands on each clock to show the time.

1. quarter past 2:00          2. quarter past 5:00          3. 8:15

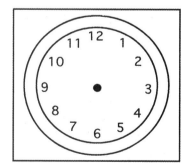

4. quarter past 10:00          5. 3:15          6. 12:15

# Three Different Ways

There are three ways to write 1:15.

1:15

15 minutes after 1

quarter after 1

Circle the time that each clock shows.

1.

quarter after 3

quarter after 6

quarter after 8

2.

15 minutes after 9

15 minutes after 12

15 minutes after 3

3.

2:15

10:15

11:15

4. Write the time the clock shows in three different ways.

_____

_____

_____

# Forty-Five After

When the long hand (minute hand) points to the 9, it is forty-five minutes after the hour.

This clock shows that it is seven forty-five. The short hand (hour hand) points to just before the next hour.

Draw the minute hand on each clock to show the time.

1.

ten forty-five

2.

one forty-five

3.

eleven forty-five

# Quarter To

Time at forty-five minutes after the hour can be written in different ways.

3:45

quarter to 4

15 minutes to 4

Circle the matching times in each row.

1.  10:45            ten forty-five            quarter to ten

2.  6:45             quarter past six          quarter to seven

3.  12:45            twelve forty-five          quarter past twelve

4.  8:45             eight forty-five          quarter past eight

5.  2:45             quarter to three          quarter past two

6.  Write the time the clock shows in three different ways.

_____

_____

_____

# Digital Clock

A digital clock does not use hands but only numbers to show the time. The number before the dots (:) shows the hour. The number after the dots shows how many minutes after (or past) the hour.

The digital clock shows that it is four fifteen.

Circle the time that each clock shows.

1.      three thirty
three fifteen
three o'clock

2.      three o'clock
three fifteen
half past three

Draw lines to connect the clocks that show the same times.

3.

4.

5.

6.

7.

8.

## Counting by Fives

*Materials: Judy Clock*

Use the Judy Clock to demonstrate that it takes five minutes for the minute hand to move from one number to the next. Have students start at the 12 and count by fives as you move the minute hand around the clock until you reach 12 again. Explain that when the minute hand is on the 1, it is five minutes after the hour; when the minute hand is on the 2, it is ten minutes after the hour; and so on.

Play this interactive game to reinforce where the minute hand points when counting by fives. Have students close their eyes. Set the Judy Clock to a time on the hour. Tell students, "It is now (name the hour)." Begin counting by fives and stop at one of the numbers. Ask, "Who knows where the minute hand is pointing?" Tell students to keep their eyes closed and try to answer. After a student guesses, ask students if they agree ("thumbs-up") or disagree ("thumbs-down") with the guess. Have students open their eyes to check the guess. If correct, have the student perform your role by setting the Judy Clock on the hour and moving the minute hand while counting aloud by fives.

## Boards Up!

*Materials: Judy Clock; write-on/wipe-away boards, markers, erasers*

This game gives students practice in writing times in five-minute intervals. Show students how to correctly write time using a colon (for example, 5:15). Give each student a board, a marker, and an eraser. Hold the Judy Clock and move the hands to show a time such as 4:05. Write the time on the board. Have students copy the time. Then, set the Judy Clock to another time. Ask students to write the time on their boards and call out, "Boards up!" when they are done. Have students hold up their boards so that you can check their answers.

As the game progresses, challenge students by giving them less and less time to write the times.

## Let's Practice!

*Materials: Judy Clock*

Explain to students that when telling time it helps to count by fives. Hold the Judy Clock. Point to and say each large number, starting with 1. Demonstrate that it takes five minutes for the minute hand to get to each large number on the clock. Help students practice counting by fives. Then, ask students to count by fives as you move the minute hand from one number to the next.

# Floor Clock

*Materials: Judy Clock, 12 rubber pads, marker*

This activity allows students the opportunity to get a "physical" sense of time. Number the pads 1 to 12 like the numbers on a clock face. Then, make a floor clock by placing the pads on the floor facedown so that students will not be confused, for example, by the number 4 representing "20." Use the floor clock for the following time games:

**Walk the Clock**

Tell students that an hour has 60 minutes. Ask students to take turns walking slowly around the clock face as you count to 60, making sure that each student is at each five-minute mark at the correct time (5, 10, 15, etc.).

**Finding Fives**

Instead of counting by ones to 60, count by fives to 60. Invite volunteers to "hop" onto each pad as you count by fives together, moving around the clock face. When students seem comfortable with fives around the clock face, turn the pads over so that the numbers are showing.

# Route 60

*Materials: sidewalk chalk, copies of the Route 60 Cards (page 18), basket*

If permitted at your school, set up a winding "road" on the playground. Use colorful chalk to write large numbers (5, 10, 15, and so on to 60) at equal distances along the road. Tell students to pretend they will be driving along Route 60. Copy and laminate the cards. Cut them apart and place them in a basket. Have students sit along both sides of the route. Choose two students to be the first "drivers" and have them stand before the number 5. Let each driver choose a Route 60 card and follow the directions on the card. Each driver begins with the number she is standing on and skip counts by fives as directed on the card. The driver

travels along the route to the ending number (for example, if a driver standing on the number 10 picks a card that says, *Count by 5s three times*, the driver says aloud, "Ten, fifteen, twenty" and then stays on the number 20). The drivers continue moving along the route this way until one driver reaches 60. The first driver to reach 60 wins.

# Route 60 Cards

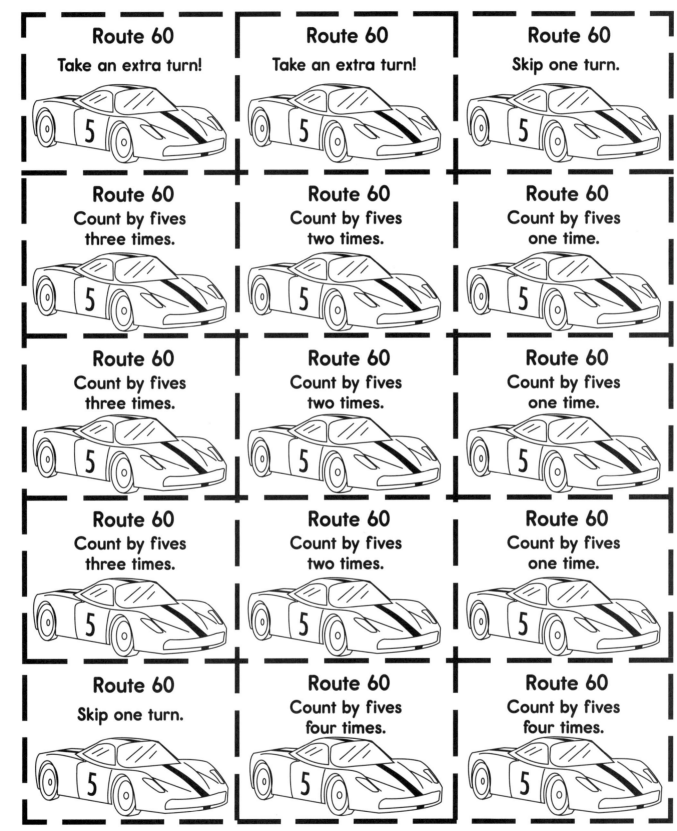

**Route 60**

Take an extra turn!

**Route 60**

Take an extra turn!

**Route 60**

Skip one turn.

**Route 60**

Count by fives
three times.

**Route 60**

Count by fives
two times.

**Route 60**

Count by fives
one time.

**Route 60**

Count by fives
three times.

**Route 60**

Count by fives
two times.

**Route 60**

Count by fives
one time.

**Route 60**

Count by fives
three times.

**Route 60**

Count by fives
two times.

**Route 60**

Count by fives
one time.

**Route 60**

Skip one turn.

**Route 60**

Count by fives
four times.

**Route 60**

Count by fives
four times.

# Race around the Clock

*Materials: Judy Clock, sidewalk chalk*

Reinforce counting by fives with this lively activity. If permitted at your school, use chalk to draw a large clock on the playground. Using the Judy Clock as a guide, write the smaller numbers (5, 10, 15, and so on to 60) next to their corresponding numbers on the playground clock. Have students sit in pairs at each smaller number around the outside of the clock. Hold the Judy Clock. Choose two students—one to be the "racer" and the other to be the "caller." Explain how Race around the Clock works (it is similar to Duck, Duck, Goose). The racer stands on the outside of the circle by the number 60. The caller moves the minute hand around the Judy Clock, loudly counting by fives as the racer moves to each pair of students. When the caller yells, "Stop," the racer taps the students at that number. The tapped students quickly get up and race around the outside of the clock, trying to tag the racer. If the racer gets to the empty spot before being tapped, the racer and the caller take that spot and the players who were tapped are the new racer and caller. If the racer is tagged, the caller and the racer switch roles.

# What's My Number?

*Materials: Judy Clock*

Hold the Judy Clock. Point out each large number, starting with 1. Show how it takes five minutes for the minute hand to move to each large number on the clock. Help students practice counting by fives as you move the minute hand around the clock.

Then, turn the Judy Clock face toward you and move the minute hand to the number 3. Say to students, "I see a number inside a circle by the three. What's my number?" To check an answer, turn the Judy Clock around for the class to see. Continue this activity until you have covered all of the numbers. Challenge students by moving randomly around the clock.

# Countdown

*Materials: Judy Clock, copies of the* Task Cards *(pages 21–22)*

Countdown provides a fun way to reinforce counting by fives around the clock. Give each student one card. Then, set the Judy Clock to a time on the hour. Invite students to take turns performing their tasks for the class. When a student begins, the rest of the class calls out, "Countdown!" Students count aloud by fives while you move the minute hand around the clock. As soon as a student completes a task, ask a volunteer to read the time on the Judy Clock.

You may also use the Task Cards to fill extra class time. If you have an extra five or ten minutes, let a student choose a card. The rest of the class counts to see how long it takes for that student to complete the task.

Countdown can be played without Task Cards too. While students are cleaning up, lining up, getting drinks, and so on, have everyone count to see how long each task takes.

# Match It! Game

*Materials: Judy Clock, copies of the* Match It! Game Cards *(pages 23–24)*

Laminate and cut apart the game cards. Place them in a learning center with the Judy Clock. Have two students at a time play this game (it is similar to Concentration). Have players lay the Match It! Game Cards facedown in rows. The first player turns over two cards. If the times match, the player must read the time and set the Judy Clock to match. The player then keeps the two cards. If the player reads the time or sets the Judy Clock incorrectly, the player must return the cards to their original places. The player must also return the cards if they do not match. The player with the most cards at the end wins.

# Task Cards

Write your full address.

Draw a picture of your house.

Stand and do 25 toe touches.

Untie and tie a shoe.

Toss and catch a ball 10 times.

Clap 50 times.

Blow up a balloon.

Bounce a ball 20 times.

Do 40 jumping jacks.

# Task Cards

Do 10 crab-walk steps.

Draw 10 hearts.

Wink 30 times.

Call out the name of each classmate.

Cut out a large paper circle.

Blink 30 times.

Twirl around 10 times.

Roll a number cube 20 times.

Cut out a large paper rectangle.

# Match It! Game Cards

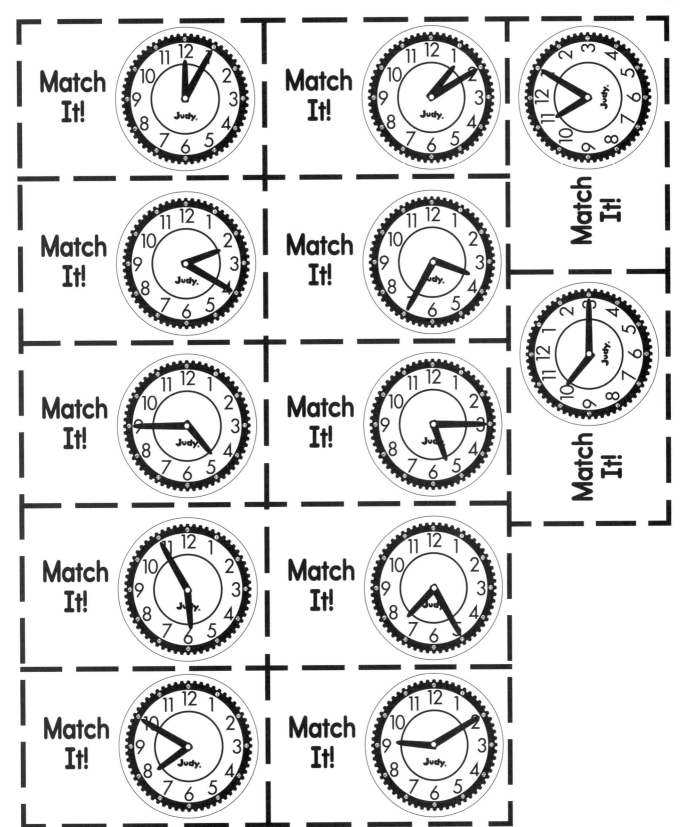

## Match It! Game Cards

**Match It!**
5 minutes after 12

**Match It!**
10 minutes after 1

**Match It!**
5 minutes after 11

**Match It!**
20 minutes after 2

**Match It!**
35 minutes after 3

**Match It!**
15 minutes after 10

**Match It!**
45 minutes after 4

**Match It!**
15 minutes after 5

**Match It!**
55 minutes after 6

**Match It!**
25 minutes after 7

**Match It!**
50 minutes after 8

**Match It!**
10 minutes after 9

# Time Match Game

*Materials: Judy Clock, copies of the Time Match Game Board and Time Match Game Cards (pages 26–28), number cube, game tokens*

This fun center game for two to four players lets students practice matching time on digital and analog clocks. Color and laminate the game board and the cards for extended use and then cut apart the cards.

Place the Judy Clock, a number cube, game tokens (for example, buttons or beans), the game board, and the game cards on a table in a learning center. Have students place the game cards facedown in rows in front of them. To begin, each player places a token on *Entrance* on the game board. Players then take turns rolling the number cube. The first player moves her token the number of spaces. Then, the player follows the directions on the space she lands on.

If the directions read *Pick 2 cards*, then the player turns over two cards. If the times on the cards match, the player must set the Judy Clock to that time correctly to keep the two cards. (Remind students that matching cards show the same time on an analog clock and a digital clock.) If the times do not match, the player returns the cards facedown. Then, it is the next player's turn. The object is to move along the path from *Entrance* to *Exit*. When a player reaches *Exit* with an exact roll, the game is over. Players then count their cards. The player with the most cards wins.

# Time Match Game Board

**Entrance**

Pick 2 cards.

Pick 2 cards.

Stop to eat. Lose a turn.

Pick 4 cards.

Win the ring toss! Move ahead 1 space.

Pick 2 cards.

Pick 2 cards.

Wait in line. Lose a turn.

Pick 2 cards.

Ride closed. Go back 2 spaces.

Take a pony ride. Go ahead 1 space.

Pick 4 cards.

Pick 2 cards.

Pick 2 cards.

**Exit**

# Time Match Game Cards

# Time Match Game Cards

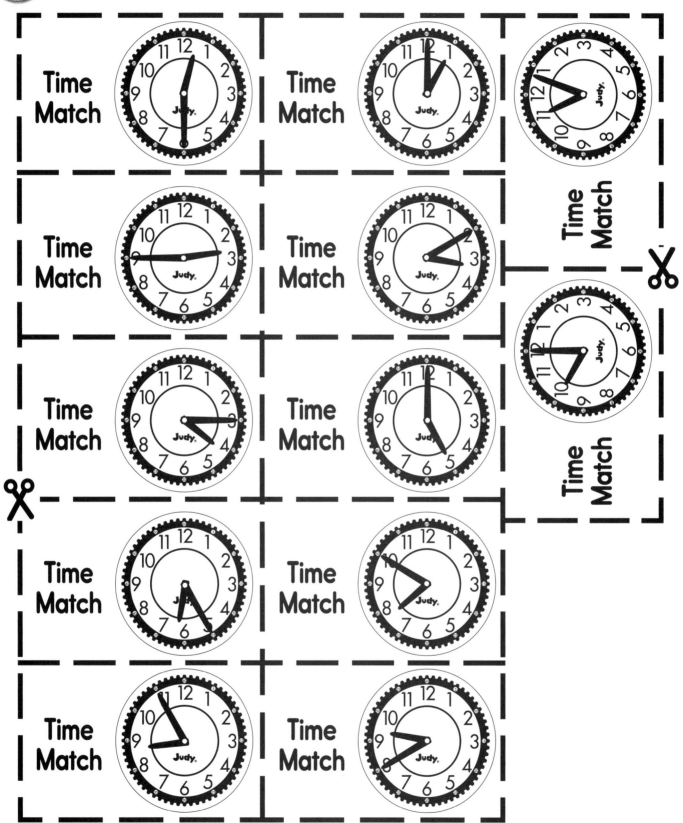

Time Match

Time Match

Time Match

Time Match

Time Match

Time Match

Time Match

Time Match

Time Match

Time Match

Time Match

Time Match

## Counting by Fives

To tell time, it helps to be able to count by fives. Practice counting by fives a few times.

5, 10, 15, 20, 25, 30, 35, 40, 45, 50, 55, 60

Close your eyes and try it again. Did you get it right? If not, keep practicing.

Look at the clock. Point to each number, starting at 1. Count by fives. When you get to the 12, you should be back at 60. It takes 5 minutes for the minute hand to get to each number on the clock.

What number is in the circle by the 3? _____

What number is in the circle by the 6? _____

What number is in the circle by the 8? _____

What number is in the circle by the 11? _____

Write the missing numbers in the circles on the clock. Remember to count by fives.

Write the missing numbers.

1.  5 _____ 15 _____ 25 _____ 35 _____ 45 _____ 55 _____

2.  _____ 10 15 20 _____ _____ 35 40 45 50 _____ 60

3.  5 _____ _____ _____ 25 _____ _____ 40 45 _____ _____ _____

# How about the I and the 2?

You know how to read a clock when the minute hand points to the 12, the 3, the 6, and the 9. Learning the rest of the numbers is easy!

When the minute hand is on the I, it is 5 minutes after the hour. 4:05 means the same as 5 minutes after 4.

When the minute hand is on the 2, it is 10 minutes after the hour. 4:10 means the same as 10 minutes after 4.

Write the time shown on each clock.

1.

2.

3.

4.

_____   _____   _____   _____

Draw both hands on each clock to show the time.

5.

6.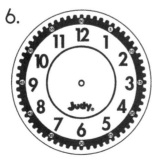

7.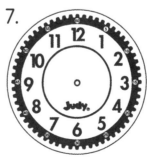

8.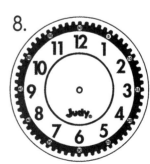

10 minutes after I

5 minutes after 10

10 minutes after 12

5 minutes after 2

# Now You're Ready for the 4 and the 5

Count by fives to the 4 and the 5. Start at the 12.

0, 5, 10, 15, 20, 25

When the minute hand is on the 4, it is 20 minutes after the hour. 4:20 means the same as 20 minutes after 4.

When the minute hand is on the 5, it is 25 minutes after the hour. 4:25 means the same as 25 minutes after 4.

Draw both hands on each clock to show the time.

1.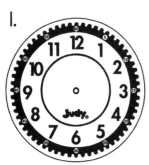

20 minutes after 10

2.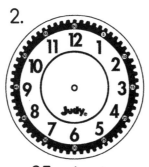

25 minutes after 11

3.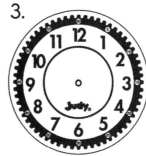

25 minutes after 3

4.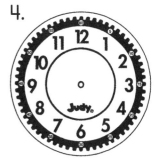

20 minutes after 8

Write the time shown on each clock.

5.

6.

7.

8.

_____   _____   _____   _____

# 7 and 8—It's Getting Late

When the minute hand has passed the 6, it is on its way to the next "o'clock." Look at the hour hand. It is getting closer to the 5.

4:35
35 minutes after 4
25 minutes to 5

When the minute hand is on the 7, it is 35 minutes after the hour. It is also 25 minutes before the next hour.

4:40
40 minutes after 4
20 minutes to 5

When the minute hand is on the 8, it is 40 minutes after the hour. It is also 20 minutes before the next hour.

Write the time shown on each clock.

1.

2.

3.

4.

_____    _____    _____    _____

Draw both hands on each clock to show the time.

5.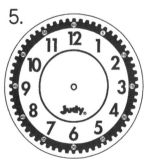

6.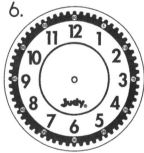

7.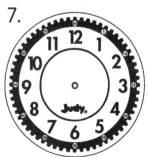

8.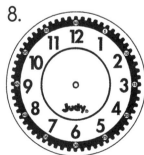

35 minutes
after 2

20 minutes
to 9

25 minutes
to 5

40 minutes
after 7

# 10 and 11—That's All, Folks!

The hour hand has moved almost to the 5. It is almost 5 o'clock.

4:50
50 minutes after 4
10 minutes to 5

When the minute hand is on the 10, it is 50 minutes after the hour. It is also 10 minutes before the next hour.

4:55
55 minutes after 4
5 minutes to 5

When the minute hand is on the 11, it is 55 minutes after the hour. It is also 5 minutes before the next hour.

Write the time shown on each clock.

1.   2.  3.  4.

_____  _____  _____  _____

Draw both hands on each clock to show the time.

5. 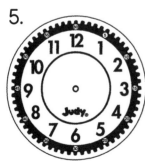  6. 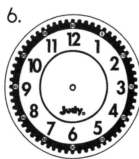  7. 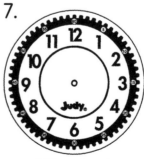  8.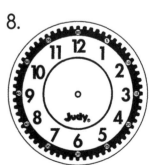

10 minutes
to 1

5 minutes
to 4

50 minutes
after 7

55 minutes
after 12

# Batty Fives

Start at 1:00 and connect the dots in order.

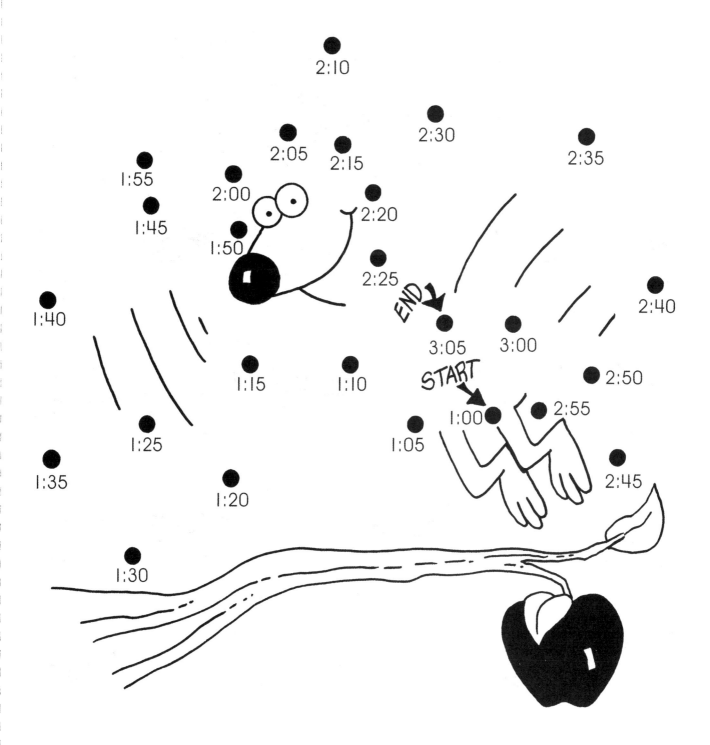

## It's About Time

Color the clock in each row that shows the correct time.

1. 10 minutes to three

2. 25 minutes after one

3. five minutes after 10

4. nine forty

5. 50 minutes after 11

6. 10:35

## The Time Is Right

Does the time match the clock? Circle *Yes* or *No*. If it does not match, write the correct time.

1.

11:15

Yes          No

_____

2.

12:55

Yes          No

_____

3.

6:20

Yes          No

_____

4.

9:25

Yes          No

_____

5.

7:50

Yes          No

_____

6.

5:40

Yes          No

_____

7.

4:35

Yes          No

_____

8.

1:10

Yes          No

_____

9.

3:05

Yes          No

_____

# Before Noon or After Noon?

*Materials: Judy Clock*

Introduce the concepts of "before noon" and "after noon." Begin by setting the Judy Clock to a time on the hour such as 9:00. Then, ask students, "If the clock shows 9:00, how do we know if it is time to go to school or time to go to bed?" Review with students the abbreviations *am* and *pm*. Tell students that *am* is short for the Latin phrase *ante meridiem*, which means "before noon." Explain that the times from midnight to before noon are followed by the abbreviation *am*. Tell students that a helpful way to remember *am* is the phrase "after midnight." Tell students that *pm* is short for the Latin phrase *post meridiem*, which means "after noon." Invite students to practice these concepts by playing this interactive game. Set the Judy Clock to a time. Say to students, "I eat breakfast at this time. Is it am or pm?" Repeat the activity several times. Challenge students to come up with their own am and pm questions for classmates to answer.

# Writing Times

*Materials: Judy Clock; write-on/wipe-away boards, markers, erasers*

Give students practice writing am and pm times. Give each student a board, a marker, and an eraser. Set the Judy Clock to a time such as 7:40. Say to students, "How would you write 20 minutes to 8 in the morning?" Encourage students to write the correct time followed by *am* or *pm* and hold up their boards for you to check. Ask volunteers to share their answers. Repeat the game several times.

# AM and PM Hands

*Materials: Judy Clock, washable markers, index cards (optional)*

Help students understand *am* and *pm* by reviewing the concepts of day and night. Remind students that each day is made up of 24 hours. Tell students that the way to let people know if the clock says 7 o'clock in the morning or 7 o'clock at night is to say *am* or *pm* after the time. To demonstrate this, set the Judy Clock to 7 o'clock and say, "The time is 7 o'clock am. It is 7 o'clock in the morning." Tell students that *am* means "early in the day or before noon." Move the minute hand around the clock until you come to 7 o'clock again and say, "The time now is 7 o'clock pm. It is 7 o'clock at night." Tell students that *pm* means "after noon or the time between noon and midnight."

Have each student use a washable marker and write *am* on one hand (or index card) and *pm* on the other hand (or index card). Set the Judy Clock to a time such as 8 o'clock. Say to students, "It is 8 o'clock. I am eating breakfast. Is it am or pm?" Students should raise one of their hands in response. Set the clock again and repeat the activity several times.

Challenge students by telling them you might call out an activity that is done both during the day and at night such as brushing teeth. Tell students that if you do call out this kind of activity, they should hold up both am and pm hands.

# Picture Perfect

*Materials: Judy Clock, paper, crayons or markers*

Invite students to draw two pictures each—one that shows something done during the day and one that shows something done at night. Divide students into small groups. Have them take turns sharing their pictures within the groups. Ask them to work as groups to guess the time each activity takes place and show the time on their Judy Clocks. For example, a student could draw the following:

- Picture of a student walking a dog (8 o'clock in the morning)
- Picture of a student in pajamas, brushing teeth (9 o'clock at night)

After everyone has a chance to share their pictures and discuss the times, talk about the designations of *am* and *pm*. Tell students that *am* means "early in the day" (morning and early afternoon), and *pm* means "later in the day" (late afternoon and nighttime). The clock can show 8:00 in the morning and 8:00 in the evening. Guide students to see that even though a clock may show the same time, it could be morning or night.

# AM/PM Matchup

*Materials: Judy Clock, index cards, marker*

Students will match times of day with activities in this silent game. On separate index cards, print *am*, *pm*, and *am/pm*. Make enough cards so that half of the class has one card each. Ask half of the class to stand on one side of the room. Then, tape a card to the back of each student so that he cannot see it. Then, on separate index cards, print phrases that describe activities done in the morning, in the evening, or both in the morning and the evening (for example, eat breakfast, eat dinner, wake up, go to bed, brush hair, brush teeth). Tape an activity card to the back of each student in the other half of the class. Each student then tries to find a partner—someone who matches his time of day and/or night with a corresponding activity. For example, a student wearing an *am* card needs to find someone wearing a morning activity card. Students can help each other find partners by nodding yes or no or by using their hands to move "matches" together. Partners should then stand next to each other. The game is over when everyone finds a match. Challenge the class by setting a time limit.

## AM or PM?

Write *am* or *pm* after each time.

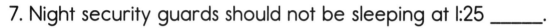

1. Most people eat breakfast at about 8:00 _____.

2. The evening news starts at 6:00 _____.

3. Morning cartoons start at 5:30 _____.

4. School starts at 8:30 _____.

5. School is over at 3:30 _____.

6. The sun probably is not shining at 11:15 _____.

7. Night security guards should not be sleeping at 1:25 _____.

8. Many young children take afternoon naps at about 2:00 _____.

Circle either *am* or *pm* to name the time of day for each activity.

| | | |
|---|---|---|
| 9. eat breakfast | am | pm |
| 10. go to school | am | pm |
| 11. eat dinner | am | pm |
| 12. go to bed | am | pm |
| 13. watch the sunrise | am | pm |

Write each time, including *am* or *pm*.

14. Ten o'clock in the morning. _____

15. Fifteen minutes after one in the afternoon. _____

16. Thirty minutes after six in the evening. _____

17. Twenty minutes to nine in the morning. _____

18. Five minutes to eleven in the evening. _____

# Clothespin Clock Stoppers

*Materials: Judy Clock, clothespins, red and green markers*

Introduce elapsed time and help students practice counting by fives with this game. Find two spring-activated clothespins. Mark one red and one green. Ask a student to set the Judy Clock to a time on the hour and clip the green clothespin onto the clock so that it points to the 12. Ask another student to clip the red clothespin onto the Judy Clock so that it points to a large number on the clock. With the class, count by fives from the green clothespin to the red. Ask, "How much time went by? What time did we start counting? What time did we stop counting?" Move the minute hand from the 12 to where the red clothespin is clipped and let students count again.

# Counting Time

*Materials: Judy Clock; write-on/wipe-away boards, markers, erasers*

Give each student a board, a marker, and an eraser. Set the Judy Clock to a time. Have students write the time and hold up their boards for you to check. Then, say something such as, "Add ten minutes." Have students write the new time and hold up their boards again for you to check. Choose students to set the Judy Clock to the new time. Encourage students to count the time as the minute hand is moving. They may count by ones or fives, depending on the passage of time. Based on students' skills, you may want to vary this game by having students subtract time. Say something such as, "Subtract one hour" or "Subtract five minutes."

# Mental Math

*Materials: Judy Clock*

Give students a lot of mental practice on elapsed time. Have them sit around you as you hold the Judy Clock. Choose one student at a time to solve time story problems by setting the clock to starting and ending times. Present simple problems such as these:

- *Anna leaves her house at 10:00. It takes her 15 minutes to ride her bike to Cara's house. What time will Anna arrive? (10:15)*
- *Taron ate lunch at 12:00. A half hour later, he went outside to play. What time did he start playing? (12:30)*
- *Dad leaves for work at 7:00. He gets to work in 45 minutes. What time does he get to work? (7:45)*

# Passing Time

*Materials: Judy Clock*

Make up simple story problems that involve the passage of time—either by the hour or the half hour. For each problem, set the Judy Clock at the beginning time. After students listen to each story problem, have them take turns moving the hands on the Judy Clock to show the solutions to the problems. Present problems such as these:

- *Tyler eats breakfast at 7:00 in the morning. (Set the Judy Clock to 7:00.) The school bus comes to the bus stop 30 minutes later. What time does Tyler have to be at the bus stop? (7:30)*
- *Lily has lunch at 12:30 at school. (Set the Judy Clock to 12:30.) She has music 1 hour before lunch. What time does she have music? (11:30)*
- *Ben had soccer practice for 1 hour. (Set the Judy Clock to 3:00.) If it started at 3:00, what time did soccer practice end? (4:00)*
- *Shannon's favorite TV show starts at 6:30. (Set the Judy Clock to 6:30.) It lasts for 30 minutes. What time is the TV show over? (7:00)*

As students master this activity, let them come up with their own story problems to provide a fun way to practice elapsed time.

# Caring for Pets

Complete the time chart. Use a clock to help you.

| Job | Starts | Ends | Time |
|---|---|---|---|
| | 8:30 | _____ | 30 minutes |
| | 9:00 | _____ | 1 hour |
| | _____ | 10:30 | 30 minutes |
| | _____ | 11:15 | 15 minutes |

## Time Going By

1. Look at the clock. What time will it be . . .

in 20 minutes? _____

in 5 minutes? _____

in 1 hour? _____

in 2 hours? _____

Look at the two clocks. How much time has gone by?

2. 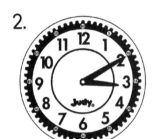  _____ minutes

3.   _____ minutes

4. 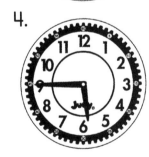  _____ minutes

5.   _____ minutes

# Adding and Subtracting Time

Complete the time charts.

### 1. Add 20 minutes.

| 6:00 | ____ : _____ |
|------|-------------------|
| 8:30 | ____ : _____ |
| 2:25 | ____ : _____ |

### 2. Add 5 minutes.

| 4:10 | ____ : _____ |
|------|-------------------|
| 6:15 | ____ : _____ |
| 3:55 | ____ : _____ |

### 3. Subtract 2 hours.

| 10:00 | ____ : _____ |
|-------|-------------------|
| 9:30  | ____ : _____ |
| 1:15  | ____ : _____ |

### 4. Add 35 minutes.

| 6:05  | ____ : _____ |
|-------|-------------------|
| 10:55 | ____ : _____ |
| 8:25  | ____ : _____ |

### 5. Subtract 15 minutes.

| 11:55 | ____ : _____ |
|-------|-------------------|
| 12:05 | ____ : _____ |
| 10:10 | ____ : _____ |

### 6. Add 3 hours.

| 11:20 | ____ : _____ |
|-------|-------------------|
| 5:35  | ____ : _____ |
| 7:05  | ____ : _____ |

# Time Tales

Solve each problem.

| | | |
|---|---|---|
| 1. Fiona left for school at 7:00 am. She got to school a half hour later. What time did she get to school? | 2. Byron's baseball game started at 1:30. It ended 2 hours later. What time did the baseball game end? | 3. Cory went to the movies at 6:00. The movie was 1 hour and 45 minutes long. What time was the movie over? |
| 4. Brianna's beach party lasted for 3 hours. It started at 1:15. What time did the beach party end? | 5. Mia's soccer game ended at 4:00. It started 50 minutes earlier. What time did the soccer game start? | 6. Stephanie's swim meet started at 2:00 pm. It ended 1 hour and 30 minutes later. What time did the swim meet end? |
| 7. Kevin jogs every morning. He starts at 5:45 am and gets home 1 hour later. What time does he get home? | 8. Mona works a 3-hour shift each day at the neighborhood pool. Her shift begins at 4:30. What time does her shift end? | 9. Carlos loves working at the animal shelter each day. His shift ends at 1:00. If he works for 2 hours, what time does his shift begin? |